Sweet, Sweet Singletrack

Written and Illustrated by Andrea Cacek

Dedicated to the place where adventure and kindness are one.

Hey!

You Ready?

TRAIL RULES

* Stay on the trails.
* Muddy trails are too wet to ride.
* Pack it in, pack it out!
* Stay in control of your bike.
* Step aside for non-bikers and bikers going uphill.
* Slow down for four-leggeds.
* HAVE FUN!

Ready!

Let's SHRED!

Hey!

You Ready?

Made in the USA
Lexington, KY
26 March 2018